Fixing and Skating with In-line and Roller Skates

Fixing and Skating with In-line and Roller Skates

Russell J. Terry

"Relaxing Russ"

VANTAGE PRESS
New York

FIRST EDITION

Copyright © 1997 by Russell J. Terry

Published by Vantage Press, Inc.
516 West 34th Street, New York, New York 10001

Manufactured in the United States of America
ISBN: 0-533-11983-9

Library of Congress Catalog Card No.: 96-90272

0 9 8 7 6 5 4 3 2 1

To those who want to skate

Contents

Preface

I have spent about thirty-five years in roller rinks in mid-Michigan. Some of these rinks have since closed, like the ones in Chesaning, Durand, the Chateau in Owosso, Lansing, Charlotte, Fenmore, and one near East Lansing. But I still skate mostly at Edra in Holt. Others at Mount Morris, Owosso, Lapeer, Saint Johns, Flint, and Saginaw.

Many people have expressed to me their feelings on how they wished that they could roller skate. I plan on not only providing sketches on how to skate and explaining what to do but, just as important, informing readers how to clean and adjust their skates so that they can perform much better. You could be the best skater in the world, but without keeping your skates in good working condition, you might lose a wheel or a toe stop. This might cause you to fall and hurt yourself, or others.

Also, by doing your own work on your skates, you will know what needs to be done to your skates by the way the they respond. An example is that when it's harder for you to skate the wheels need lubrication.

Some people try to learn to skate by watching others, but the skaters do not explain how they push with their feet or shift their weight. So when they try, it's "easier said than done." But *you* can learn to skate.

It is to those who want to learn how to skate that I dedicate this book. If you want to learn how to skate, you can. It takes both time and practice, if you want to skate well. You can learn to skate in a short time, but to do the fancy tricks will require much more time and practice. Maybe even years.

I wish to thank my father and mother, Russell Ray and Alberta Terry, for buying me sidewalk roller skates when I was in school so that I could learn the basics of roller skating. Also my brother Chester, who encouraged me to do better with his skating ability. Plus, he taught me the different parts of the roller skate. To Danny Hathoway and Brian Dilian, I give thanks for taking pictures of me with an 8-mm movie camera to help me in the sketching part. "Thanks" also go to Mr. and Mrs. Orin Huffman for the use of their typewriter when I started this book about ten years ago.

And a very special thanks goes to a group of people that we Americans many times forget. Without them, this country would not be free today. They are the people who have fought and died to keep America free. I believe that the thanks to this group is not out of place.

Author's Note

With the economy as it is, many people would like to know how to lubricate their in-line or roller skates. Some would even skate, if they knew how to move their feet.

I have been skating in mid-Michigan for about thirty-five years.

Author's Note

Fixing and Skating with In-line and Roller Skates

1

Should I Buy Skates?

If you, or someone you know, wants to skate and wants to buy their own, I would suggest that you try skating a few times first before you buy. Let me illustrate this point that actually happened several years ago. I went to a church roller skating party with one of my cousins. She saw others and myself roller skating. It looked as if it would be easy. She got so motivated that she decided to try it with one person on one side and me on the other. But when she tried to skate, it was harder than she anticipated. She made one complete circle around the floor and that ended her roller skating career. Now you can see why, if you like something, try it out before you become too involved.

Let's say that you've skated a few times and you decided that you still like it. You might have fallen down a few times, but you still believe that it's fun. But before you buy skates, try to settle two important questions in your mind first: (1) How often can I go skating? (2) Can I afford skates?

If you live within a short distance from a rink and have nothing much to do, you would have no problem about how often you can go skating because you will have a lot of time. But if you can only skate once or twice per month, then it would probably be cheaper for you to rent your skates. Although renting roller skates usually means that when you get a pair, they will skate hard, or one skate will want to go to your right while you want to go straightforward, or go around a left curve. If you won't be using your skates very much, you might not pay off your skates. To "pay off your skates" means that you write on a piece of paper how much you paid for the skates. Each time that you go roller skating, you subtract your skate rental from what you paid for your skates. Because if you didn't have your own skates, then you would have had to rent skates, and that would have cost you more money to go into the rink. When your balance is zero, then you can use the money that you save toward a new pair of skates, a bike, college, or whatever you want to do with it.

Only you can determine if you can afford skates or not! If you are a small child, maybe your parents can buy you a pair of skates that are not expensive. Keep in mind that your feet will grow. But if you have lots of money, then you can buy them new. Or maybe you can ask your parents to buy a pair, and then they could withhold a certain amount of your allowance until your parents have received their money.

Or you could make arrangements with the owner/manager at the rink. After you decide what skates you want and the total cost, inform the owner/manager how much you can afford each week or month. Then each time you give them money, get a receipt that includes the new balance of what you owe. After the skates are paid off, if they are old, they can then give them to you. If they are new, then the order can be sent to the company who makes the skates. Children should get their skates a little larger because their feet are still growing.

For those with skateboards, you can use the maintenance chapter for in-line or roller skates, whichever works best.

In-line Skates

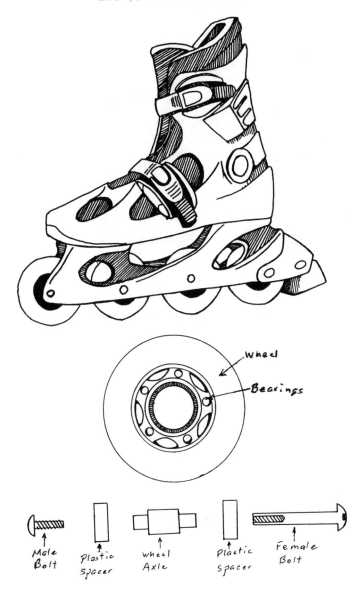

Wheel

Bearings

Male Bolt

Plastic Spacer

Wheel Axle

Plastic Spacer

Female Bolt

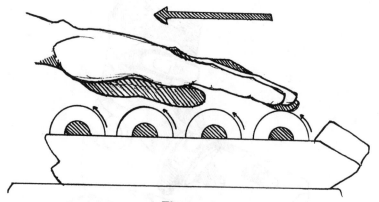

Figure 1

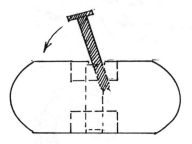

Figure 2

2

In-line Skates

Lubricating In-line Skates

Before you buy a used pair of in-line skates, with one hand, turn the skate upside down so that your wheels are up in the air, as in figure 1. If you're right-handed, hold your skate with your left hand. You will move your right arm from the left of your body to the right as in the same figure. "Spin" one wheel at a time by putting a finger on the wheel to spin it. You will do this in a fast motion. Observe the spinning of the wheel. If the wheel makes a few rotations after your finger leaves the wheel, it's probably lubricated. But if it stops, it needs to be lubricated. But if the wheel goes backwards, even 1/16th of an inch, it most likely needs to be loosened.

To be sure, ask the owner for some tools so that you can use them in his (her) presence. This is to see if the wheel is on too tight. Use one tool on the bottom bolt to prevent it from turning. Then use the other on top to turn the nut (or other half of the bolt). Turn it counterclockwise about 1/4 turn to loosen the bolt. Spin the wheel again. If it still doesn't spin, chances are the wheels need to be lubricated.

To lubricate in-line wheels:

(1) Put a piece of cloth over your work area that can be thrown away when you are done.

(2) Use an Allen wrench (need two, 5/32 inch or 4 mm), socket, or whatever you need to prevent the bottom bolt from turning. With the skate on its side, use the other tool on top of the skate and turn the bolt (nut) in a counterclockwise direc-

tion to separate the two. After removing the bolt(s), then remove the wheel.

(3) With the wheel placed flat on your work area, place a small screwdriver, nail, or Allen wrench (long part) into the bearing of the wheel, as illustrated in figure 2. Allow the tool to lay down by forcing it. This will cause that bearing to pop out. You can then take your tool to remove the bearing. Then turn the wheel upside-down and remove the other bearing the same way.

Wheels

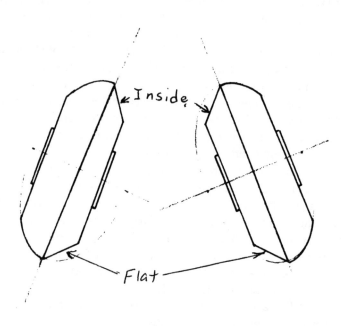

Figure 3

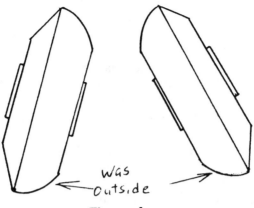

was
←Outside

Figure 4

(4) Some people lubricate with motor oil (10-30w, 20w, or whatever you have), lubricating oil, or WD-40. When you lubricate your bearings each time, you can use motor oil the first time, lubricating oil the next time, and WD-40 after that. That way you will see which works best for you. With motor and lubricating oil, start out with two drops at first, placed in the inside part of the bearing (outside of the bearing has no opening to allow the oil to go into the bearings). Then spin the bearing to spread the oil around inside the bearing. Do this to both bearings. With WD-40, spray into the inside of the bearing about two seconds with a plastic tube on the can.

(5) Figure 3 illustrates what happens to your wheels while you skate. On the inside half of the wheels, they become flat. So each time you lubricate your wheels, turn the wheels around from figure 3 to figure 4. Unless the outside of the wheel is more flat than the inside that you had skated on, put the bolt(s) through the in-line skate and wheel. Remember to use one tool under the skate to prevent the bolt from turning. With the skate on its side, tighten the top part of the bolt with the other tool. But if the top bolt (nut) turns clockwise hard, reverse the direction to get the two parts free from each other and try again.

If you force the two together, they could become cross-threaded and, in time, strip the threads. And you will have to buy a new bolt. Turning the bolt clockwise should be easy. When you feel a little resistance, you should stop. *You don't need to get the bolts very tight.* If you can use a socket extension, that's usually enough to get the bolt(s) tight enough. You can usually use the tools at a skating rink to do some adjustments. After a while, you'll get to know how much to tighten the bolt(s) for the best performance from your in-line skates.

Also, remember to check your wheels to see if oil has run down the wheel. This indicates that you have too much oil in the bearings. If none, the next time that you lubricate, try using three drops, etc. Let's say for example that no oil has leaked out on the wheels with five drops of oil. But on six drops oil has leaked out of the bearings and onto the wheels. Then you will know that you can use five drops for lubrication. You don't want the oil to leak on the wheel because then the oil will run on the floor. The oil will make that spot slippery. And someone could slip and fall and hurt themselves very badly.

3

Making a Bearing Puller for Roller Skates

You will most likely need a bearing puller for the newer plastic skating wheels. If you don't have a bearing puller, here is how you can make one. And the cost to you will be very little.

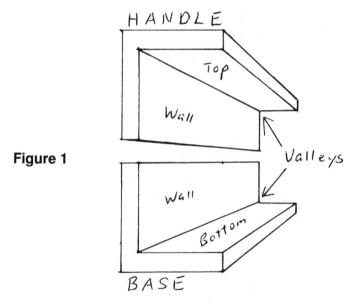

Figure 1

Acetylene Torch (Blowtorch)

(1) You first need two pieces of angle iron, as in figure #1. They should be at least one inch (top and bottom), one inch (Wall), and between six to ten inches long, plus 1/8 inch (thick).

HANDLE

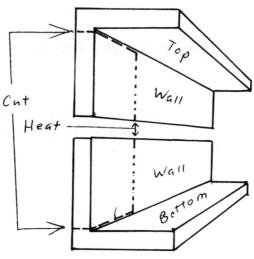

Figure 2

Base

If one angle iron is thicker than the other, use the thickest for your base, and the thinner for the handle.

(2) On the angle iron for your base, if you're right-handed, you'll be working to the left side of the iron. Use a white chalk marker to make a one-inch line along your valley that will be later *cut* by the blowtorch. And use a small T-square to make a broken line, running up the wall to indicate to *heat*. An example is found in figure #2. On the handle, also start from the left to make a chalk line of one inch long at the valley. And use the T-square to run a broken line along its wall in the same figure. Try to use a T-square that has no plastic. Plastic melts.

(3) With the bottom of your base, after starting and adjusting your torch, *cut* that one-inch line in the valley of the iron. *Make sure when you cut, the wall will clear the base when moving the wall to a 90 angle.* Then *heat* the wall where the chalk line is located. Best if the iron is in a stationary vise. One hand will hold the torch, while the other hand will use channel

locks or pliers to bend the wall, as in Figure #3-A. And use the T-square to measure the wall to make sure that it's in a 90 angle. Then *cut off* the iron that is sticking out. The iron should look like Figure #3-C. Figure #3-D shows the same idea, as if you had rolled the base toward you. Figure #4 shows you what the handle and base look like when you are done.

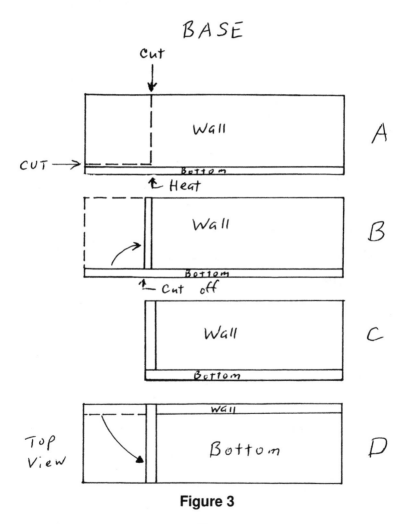

Figure 3

11

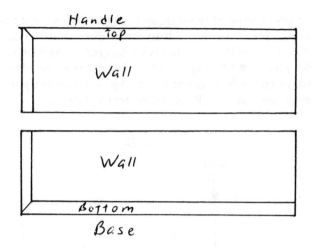

Figure 4

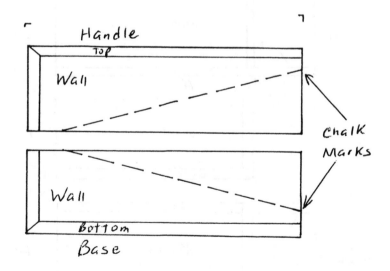

Figure 5-A

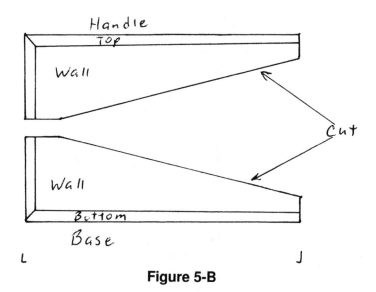

Figure 5-B

(4) In Figure #5-A, on your base, you make a chalk line from about 1/2 inch away from the iron part that you turned 90 . Then, 1/4 inch up the wall, on the handle, the mark would be down the wall. Use a ruler to make a chalk line between the two marks. Then use the torch to *cut* the chalk line so that the two angle irons resemble those of Figure #5-B. You *cut* off the iron on the base because, when you push down on the handle to remove a bearing from the roller wheel, the puller will stay flat on the table because the bottom of your base is heavier. The strip that you *cut* off the handle, is so that your handle can go down farther.

You may now go to page 17 on "Assembling the Bearing Puller."

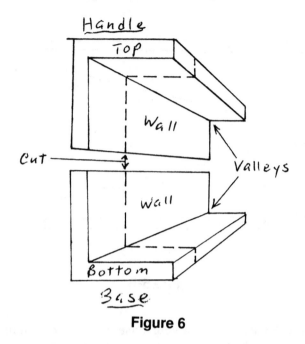

Figure 6

No Acetylene Torch (Blowtorch)

(1) You should have two pieces of angle iron at least; one inch for your walls, bottom, and top, six to ten inches long and 1/8 inch thick. If you have one angle iron thicker than the other, use your thickest for your base. Also, if you're right-handed, put the best and more accurate cut to your left. Make a one-inch chalk line in the valleys of both irons, then use a small T-square to make lines on both your base and handle, as in Figure #6. You will need a vise that is attached to a heavy workbench. Put one angle iron in the vise at a time to *cut off* that one inch piece to the left. A hacksaw would probably be the best. Also, put the longest part in the vise when cutting.

14

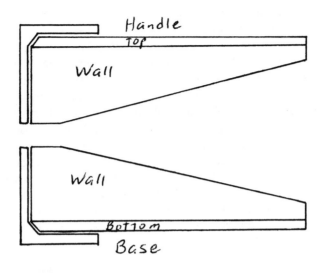

Figure 7

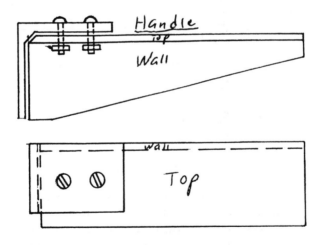

Figure 8

(2) You will have a basic idea of the locations of these two one-inch pieces of iron that had been cut in Figure #7. But also note, that, at the tip of where you cut off the one-inch iron, about 1/3 to 1/2 of it is ground or filed down. Figure #7 also illustrates that the valley of the angle iron isn't at a 90 angle, so for the "cut off" piece of iron to be more flat against the top or bottom of your puller, it would be best to grind or file down about 1/3 to 1/2 of the edge of the full length of the iron.

(3) Figure #8 shows the locations of the angle iron that was cut off, both from the top and side views, and the locations of the bolts to connect the two pieces together. There are two bolts that are side by side. Make sure these three bolts have the same size of heads for the base, because when you push down on the handle to remove the bearing, the handle of the puller will not rock as much.

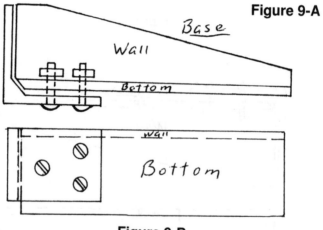

Figure 9-A

Figure 9-B

(4) In Figure #9-A, on the handle, toward where you attached the small iron, about 1/2 inch away, make a chalk mark. And about 1/8 inch down the wall, make another mark. Use a ruler to connect both marks, and make a line. Put the angle iron in your vise that is fastened to a workbench, and *cut* along that line, starting at the flat part. And *cut* to where you

attached the one-inch-long iron. The same figure shows where to put the line on your base. Figure #9-B shows what your two angle irons should look like.

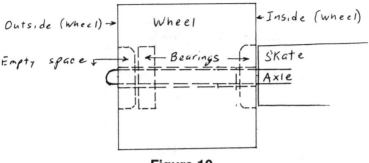

Figure 10

Assembling the Bearing Puller

(5) If your puller is about six inches long, try to find a bolt about four inches long (or shorter). The size should be about 1/4 inch, as in Figure #10. That's so that the bolt will go through the hole of the bearings, where you took the wheel off the axle of your roller skate.

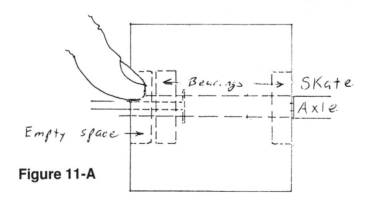

Figure 11-A

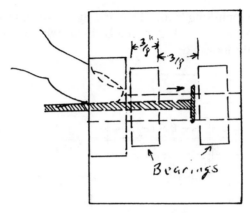

Bearings

Figure 11-B

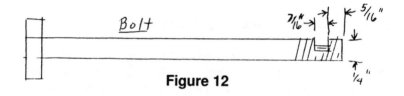

Bolt

Figure 12

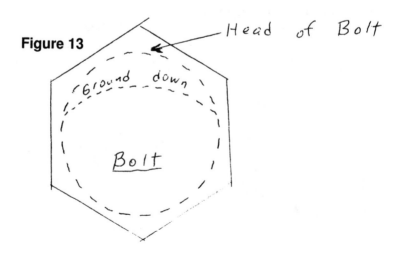

Figure 13

Head of Bolt

Ground down

Bolt

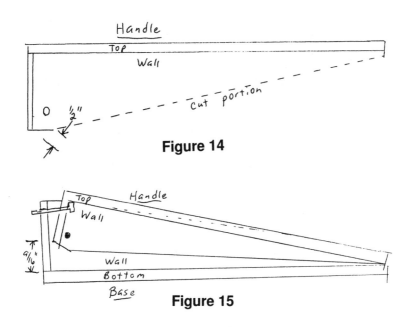

Figure 14

Figure 15

(6) You will need to know the thickness of your bearings and the space between the bearings, to measure the thickness of the bearings. Figure #11-A shows you how. Get a nail with a small enough head that can go into the hole of the bearing, but big enough, so that when you lift the nail up and pull it back, the nail will stop when the head hits the bearing and will not come out. Place your thumb of the hand that's holding the nail against the bearing, as in Figure #11-A. Take the nail out of the bearing to measure the length, then place the nail back in and let it be stopped by the other bearing. Use your thumb as a marker again. Measure the length again. If your bearing is for example 3/8 inch thick, you will need 3/8 inch or more to allow your bearing to fall into the hole that you make.

The second measurement is the length or shorter one that you need in order to allow the part that you don't file, to go between your two bearings. The example is Figure #12. If the distance between the two bearings is 3/8 inch, you make it 5/16 inch. If you grind with a 3/8 inch grinding wheel, and the bearing is 3/8 inch thick, after you have ground down about half of the bolt (making sure that basically the head is pointing up as shown in Figure #13), then push the head of the bolt toward the grinding wheel some. This way, the skating wheel with the bearing in it should drop into the slot that you have just ground-down, with a 7/16" slot on the bolt.

(7) Next select a nut and bolt that are about one inch long and at least 1/4 inch in thickness. And get a drill bit that will make a hole big enough for the bolt to go through. Then drill a hole into the handle of your puller in the basic area, as shown in Figure #14.

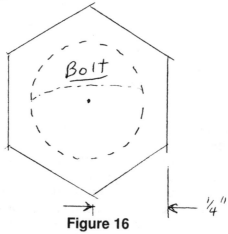

Figure 16

(8) After drilling the hole in the handle, measure the distance between that hole to the point away from the hole. Let's say for example that the largest distance of the part of the iron is 1/2 inch. Tip over the base and handle backwards so that you can raise the hole of the handle about 9/16 inch above the wall of your bottom on the base angle iron but keep an eye on the bolt. Then drag the handle backwards until you get the distance as in Figure #15. Again, pay attention to the position of the bolt, and use chalk to mark the hole on the wall of the base. Remove the handle and use a hammer and a punch to

make a dot in the center of the mark. Then drill the hole out. When you have drilled the hole, put the one-inch-long bolt through the hole of the handle. Then place a flat washer on the bolt, and slide the bolt through the wall of the base. Put the nut on back and tighten it so that the handle can be moved up and down. Make sure that the handle is in the "down" position when you do this.

(9) Now, measure the head of the bolt, as shown in Figure #16. If the distance of the center of the head on the bolt, to the outside wall is 1/4 inch, make a chalk mark of 1/32 inch farther away. This chalk mark would be on the handle. Then study where to put a chalk mark on your base, so that the two dots will be straight across. Separate the base and handle, then drill the holes after you used a punch to make a mark so that the drill bit will drill where you made the small hole with the punch. Use a drill bit that is at least 1/16 inch bigger than your bolt. If the two holes are not straight across, the puller might work anyway. The reason for having the bolt so close to the wall, is that the bolt will not turn on you when removing a bearing.

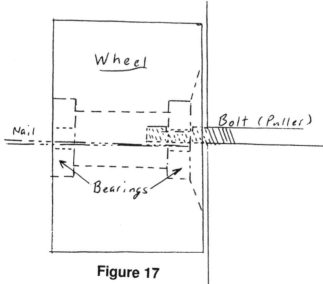

Figure 17

(10) When removing the bearing from the skate wheels, make sure that the outside of the wheel is against the wall of your puller. The outside has the bearing recessed inside the wheel. The bearing for the inside is flat with the wheel. When you lift up the handle to extend the long bolt out to have the wheel placed on the bolt, use your thumb from the hand that you are raising the handle with to push the bolt out, so that you will be able to drop the bearing on the skate wheel into the groove (ground-out) part of the bolt. Then have a small finishing nail about two inches long, as shown in Figure #17. You insert the nail at the opposite end of the skating wheel, and place the nail, under the bolt and into the inside bearing. The nail prevents the bearing from coming off the bolt, so that when you pull down on the handle, the bearing will come out.

4
Parts of the Roller Skate

Shoe

Skate Plate

Toe Stop

Support Plate
Trunk Lock Nut
Upper Trunk Washers
Upper Trunk Rubber Spacers
Front - Trunk - Rear
Lower Trunk Rubber Spacers
Lower Trunk Washers
Trunk Adjustment Bolt

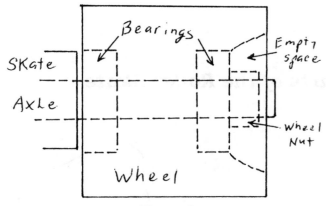

Figure 1

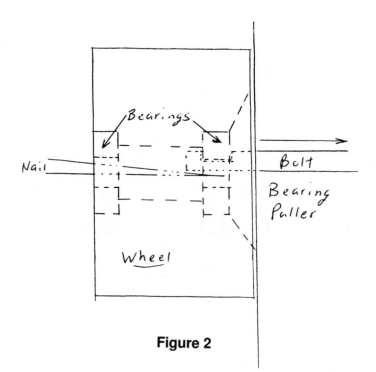

Figure 2

5

Newer Roller Skates

To work on your newer roller skates with plastic wheels, basically, you will need a bearing puller (you can make one as described in the previous chapter), a hammer, a spike nail, a finishing nail of about two inches long, a 3/4 inch bolt that's at least one inch long, an 11/16 inch (or 7mm) open-end wrench that's 5/32 inch thick (skate wrench), a 9/16 inch (or 14mm), 1/2 inch socket for 1/4 inch drive and handle, a 5/16 inch Allen wrench, lubrication, and at least a 3/8 inch thickness of plywood that measures at least two inches square with a 1 1/4 inch diameter hole in the center. Cheaper skates could vary by a bolt going through the skate wheels and trunk.

(1) First, put an old cloth over your work area. This cloth can be thrown away after you're done.

(2) Use the 1/2 inch socket with the handle to remove the wheel nut. You will turn the handle counterclockwise. Figure #1 shows how the wheel locks before you start. Please remember that the wheel nut is in the empty space in the wheel. This side of the wheel is called the outside. Remove wheel from skate.

(3) To remove the outside wheel bearing, lift up the handle on the bearing puller. And be sure to move the long bolt forward, so that it's extended out, away from the puller as indicated by the arrow for the bolt in Figure #2. You can extend the bolt with the thumb from the hand that you use to lift the handle of the bearing puller. The same figure shows that you put the outside bearing in the notch that you ground down. And the finishing nail goes through the inside bearing. Place the tip between the outside and inside bearing. The finishing nail should prevent the bolt from coming out of the bearing.

But, if somehow, the bearing doesn't come out when you force the handle down, try it again.

(4) Then turn your wheel upside down (inside of wheel, facing down) on the plywood with the hole in the center, put the head of the spike nail on the inside bearing. Tap the head of the spike nail with the hammer. You move the nail from side to side on the bearing until the bearing comes out of the wheel.

(5) Clean the tops of both sides of the bearing by going over the tops with the old cloth. Look for hairs that you want to remove. (It has nothing to do with "cleanliness is next to Godliness.") Just in case you forget which wheels you have done, the clean wheel will show you that you have worked on that wheel.

(6) My suggestion is to try different types of lubrication. In that way, you will see what works best for you. You can try motor oil, lubricating oil, WD-40, bearing grease, or petroleum jelly. When I was younger, petroleum jelly would last me three to four months before the bearings went dry. Then I would have to repack them. Now being middle-aged, I have to repack them about each month with skates that are about two years old.

If you use motor or lubricating oil, start out with two drops of oil in each bearing. Spin the bearing a little, before putting the bearing back in the wheel. This will spread the oil around. After skating, if no oil is on the wheel, try three drops in each bearing the next time. Most greases will run on your skate wheel, if you have too much. And as stated before, grease or oil on skate floors, causes accidents, but if you do use petroleum jelly, put a small amount in a small container for bearing use, because if you don't want to use the jelly as a lubricant, you can still use the rest for medical purposes. But if you pack your bearings from the container, the jelly would become contaminated with germs and shouldn't be used according to the instructions on the container.

(7) After lubricating the two bearings, place one of the bearings, on the outside of the wheel first as shown in Figure

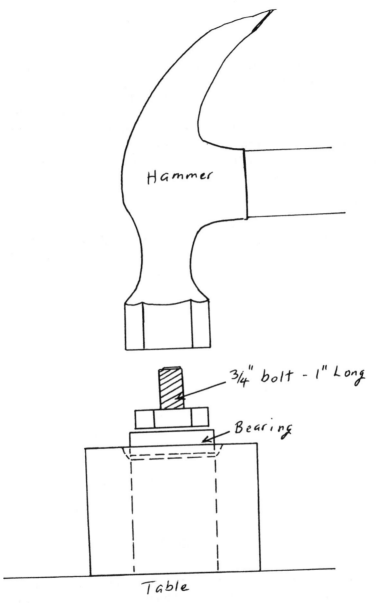

Hammer

3/4" bolt - 1" Long

Bearing

Table

Figure 3

#3. The exposed ball bearings should be facing down. This means that you put the bearings in without being able to see the ball bearings with outside of wheel up and bearing in place. Put the head of the 3/4 inch bolt on the bearing and tap the bearing into the wheel. Pay attention to the sound of the tapping. After a few taps with the hammer, you will hear a solid sound. That means that your bearing is in as far as it can go. If you try to force it in farther, you could do enough damage that you might have to buy another wheel, or bearing. So listen carefully to the sound. Once that bearing is in, turn the wheel over and install the other bearing. And listen again for the solid sound. I have tried putting the bearings in reverse order, but the bearings didn't always want to go in as easily, so it's best to install the bearings on the outside of the skate wheel first. It makes no difference if the bearing had come from the inside or outside, because they can be placed either way.

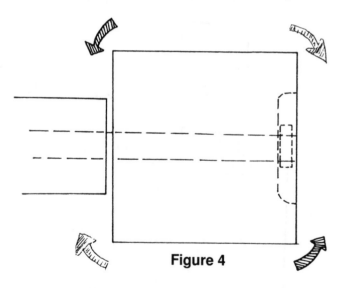

Figure 4

(8) Now place the wheel back on the skate as in Figure #1. Put the nut on also and use the 1/2 inch socket with the handle to turn the handle clockwise to tighten the bolt. When the nut

has extra resistance, stop. Take the socket off the nut. Spin the wheel. If it makes several revolutions, stop the wheel and wiggle it, as in Figure #4. Try adjusting your wheel so that it wiggles about the thickness of a hair. Turn your handle about 1/8th of a turn, until you can better judge where to set your skate adjustments. After a while, you'll know where to adjust the nut, so that you will be able to skate your best.

I'm sure that the roller rinks will allow you to use their tools to make adjustments on your skates. But if they are busy and you have to wait a few minutes for them to get the socket (wrench) for adjustments, you could take your tools and carry them in your pocket, so that while skating, you can stop off the skate floor and sit to make your adjustments. Then go back out on the floor to see if you have the proper adjustments. I have adjusted my skates as much as four times in three hours, so it's easier for me to take a socket and handle with me when I go skating.

(9) Do the same to all the other wheels.

(10) After cleaning and adjusting the last wheel, make sure that the tip of your axles have no oil or grease on them.

Tightening the Toe Stops

(11) If you can turn your toe stops with your hand, they are too loose. On the newer skates, the hex bolt to tighten the toe stop bolt is on the inside of your skates (at least with mine). With the hex bolt sticking up in the air, turn the 5/32 inch Allen wrench that's in the bolt, clockwise if the toe stop is properly lined up. If the toe stop shows wear, you could turn that flat part up before tightening the hex bolt, but if you do it to one skate, do it to the other also.

If the toe stops touch the floor most of the time while skating forwards, loosen the hex bolt with the Allen wrench, and turn the toe stop all the way into the skate, moving in a clockwise direction. Then tighten the hex bolt. Do the same with the other skate. This way, you will have to lift your heels higher in order for your toe stops to touch the floor.

I had my skates for about three months. When I could see that a metal plate was showing on my toe stops, I loosened the stops, and turned the toe stops counterclockwise so that they wouldn't rub on the floor. But that lasted for about three months, when I had to turn them again. After a year, I had the big decision to make: (1) Buy a new pair of toe stops that probably would have to be thrown out in a year's time. And buy another pair. (2) Put the toe stops that I've been using for about thirty years on my new skates, and look as if they have had very little use. These are the orange toe stops on skates that you rent at skating rinks.

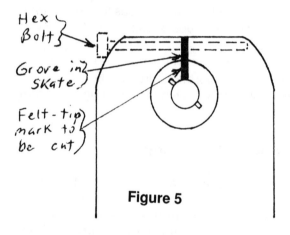

Figure 5

The problem was that the toe stop for the new skates had a thick bolt. The toe stops for my older skates had a smaller bolt. But the older skates had an adapter for the bolt. When I took the adapter out, the hole was the same size as my new skate toe stops, so I installed the adapters in the new skates. Then, with a black felt tip pen, I made a black mark from where the adapter connects with the crack in the skate, to the center of the adapter, as in Figure #5.

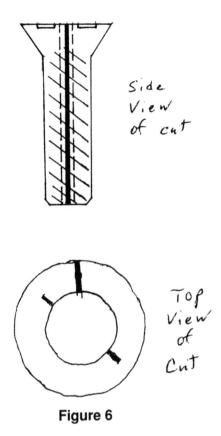

Side
View
of cut

Top
View
of
Cut

Figure 6

You could take the hex bolt out and hacksaw as much as you can to get the cut started. Then take the adapters out one at a time and use a vise or vise grips to complete the job, as in Figure #6. By cutting the adapter on the mark as shown, when you tighten the hex bolt, you force the two skate halves to crush together on the adapter halves. The adapter halves crush together on the bolt that holds the toe stop to the skate.

For the first month, when you're done skating, usually the toe stop will turn. This means it's loose. Turn your hex bolt counterclockwise to loosen it. Then check to see if you want to rotate your stops for wear in another place. For example, if the

31

stop has a flat spot on it, you might turn it a half a turn to cause wear on the opposite side. Then turn the screwdriver that is on the bolt that keeps the toe stop on the skate. When that bolt is tightened, then tighten the hex bolt. Next month, check the stops every other week, then once a month if the toe stops stay tightened.

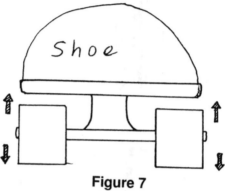

Figure 7

Adjusting the Trunks

If right-handed, hold your skate with your left hand, and with your right hand, try to wiggle the trunk as shown in figure #7. For a basic idea of where to set the trunks, you need strength to wiggle the axle and wheels. If you cannot wiggle the assembly, it's too tight. When skating, this may cause you to go straightforward when you want to turn. Or while skating, the skate might want to wander to the left or to the right. If the axle moves too easily, you will not have control of your skate, and will most likely be traveling in a pattern of a snake.

(12) Place your skate on its side. The toe stop could be facing you, or away from you. You will need a skate wrench to loosen your trunk lock nut. If a roller rink won't sell you one, you can grind down an 11/16 inch open-end wrench to a maximum of 5/32 inch thick, or until it fits on the nut. Be sure

to have a small can of water with you. After you've finished grinding, put the wrench into the water. This will bring back the temper of the wrench and your wrench will not break as easily. Bring the wrench that's on the trunk lock nut, as shown on page 23, toward you to loosen it. If the trunk is too tight, turn your screwdriver (wrench) in a counterclockwise direction. If it's too loose, turn your tool in a clockwise direction to tighten the bolt.

(13) Now, bring the skate wrench toward you to tighten the trunk lock nut.

(14) Wiggle the trunk assembly again. If it's not right, readjust it by going through the same process. The final adjustments will come when you skate.

(15) When you're done, wipe off your tools on the old cloth, and throw it away. Because you're done until the next time.

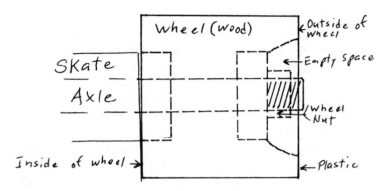

Figure 1

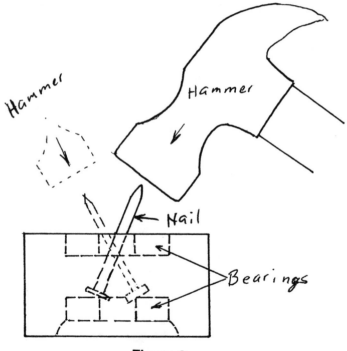

Figure 2

6

Older Skates
(With 3/8-inch Wheel Nut)

The older skates have a 3/8 inch wheel nut to hold the wheel to the skate. They usually have the old-fashioned wooden wheels. If these skates have plastic wheels, refer to the previous chapter regarding the maintenance on your skates. But take your 3/8 inch (or 10mm) socket wrench, with you.

The wooden wheels are made from hard wood. Some have some plastic on the outside part of the wheel. Without the plastic ring on the wheels, I had to have the wheels ground about every other week, when I went skating. With the plastic ring, I very seldom ground down the wheels. And when the skates were worn out, and I had to buy new skates, you could hardly tell that the wheels had been worn.

Use only wooden wheels on wooden floors. Most of the skating rinks have now a plastic coating on the floors. The wooden wheels will tear up the plastic floors. So if you have either type of wooden wheels, first find out if the rink has wooden floors. You will have better luck in finding wooden floors by calling the older rinks.

You will need these before you start: Old cloth that can be thrown away when you're done, a hammer, a spike nail, a penny nail with a head of no larger than 3/8 inch, a 3/4 inch bolt that's at least one inch long, an 11/16 inch (or 17mm) open-end wrench that's 5/32 inch thick (skate wrench), a large screwdriver to tighten your toe stops and adjust your trunk bolt, a 3/8 inch (or 10mm) socket with a handle, lubrication (oil or grease), and at least 3/8 inch thick plywood that measures at least two inches square that has a 1 1/4 inch diameter hole in the middle.

(1) Put an old piece of cloth on your work area. You should throw this away when you're done.

(2) Use your 3/8 inch socket (wrench) to take off one wheel nut at a time. (Shown in Figure #1.)

(3) Turn the wheel upside-down as in Figure #2 on cloth and hard surface. Get a penny nail with a head that can go through the hole of the inside bearing. This is where your axle was to keep the wheel on the skate. And tap on the outside bearing (going from side to side) as also shown in Figure #2. When the bearing is out, turn the wheel over to put the wheel on the plywood with a hole in the center. And tap out the inner bearing with the spike nail.

(4) Wipe off the excess lubrication on the inside and outside of each bearing. I would suggest that you try different types of lubrication. Some people like motor oil, some lubricating oil. Still others would like to use WD-40 or a petroleum jelly. When you use any lubricant, after you have finished skating, check your wheels to see if the lubrication has run on your wheels. This means that you are using too much. With oil, use two drops in each bearing, then spin the bearing to spread the oil around. If after skating, there's no oil on the wheels, next time, use three drops, etc. When you see oil on the wheels, don't use the last count, but the amount of drops before it.

When I was younger, petroleum jelly lasted me for about three to four months, then the bearings would go dry, and I would have to repack them. But first, put a small amount in a container. That's so that you don't contaminate the rest of the jelly. Once you've used petroleum jelly for bearing use, keep it for bearing use. Now being at middle age, I have to repack them about every month with skates that are about two years old.

(5) After wiping off the wheel on both the inside and outside, place your wheel flat on the table. Place one bearing on top of the wheel, with the ball bearings unseen (facing

down). Use the 3/4 inch bolt to tap the bearing in place with a hammer. Try to drive the bearing in flat, instead of one end up in the air and the other side down. After a few taps, you should bear a different sound, like a solid sound. That tells you that the bearing is in place. If you try to force it farther down, you could do damage to your wheel, or bearing. And you might have to buy another one. So listen very carefully to the sound. Then turn the wheel over and install the other bearing in the skating wheel.

(6) Clean off the trunk and axle, and remove the hairs. The hairs could slow you down, if they get into the wheel where the ball bearings are.

(7) Now put the wheel back on the axle. You may also have a "spacer" that goes between the two bearings. I had the wheel up in the air. I'd spin the wheel, and then tap it with my hand on top of the wheel until the wheel fell into place of the axle.

(8) If you have a dust collector, put it on now. If not, then put the 3/8 inch nut on. And turn clockwise.

(9) When you feel resistance on your tool, stop and remove the tool. Spin the wheel. If it makes one or two revolutions, the nut is too tight and you should loosen it about 1/4 turn. When the wheel spins freely, that's close enough. The only way to verify the adjustment is to roller skate.

(10) Do this to the rest of your wheels.

(11) To tighten the toe stops, check the toe stop to see if you would like to adjust it. For example, if one end is more flat than the other side, loosen the bolt that holds the stop to the skate, by turning the screwdriver in a counterclockwise direction. Hand-twist the toe stop to the location that you want. Then tighten the bolt by turning the screwdriver in a clockwise direction. Turn until the toe stop is tightened. Then do this to the other one too.

(12) Go to page 32 for instructions on how to "adjust your trunks."

Loose Bearing Skates

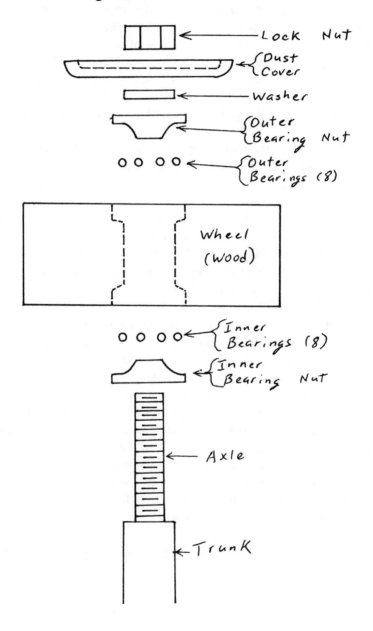

Lock Nut

Dust Cover

Washer

Outer Bearing Nut

Outer Bearings (8)

Wheel (wood)

Inner Bearings (8)

Inner Bearing Nut

Axle

Trunk

7

Loose Bearing Skates

Loose Ball Bearing Skates

Maybe one house out of one million, just might have skates that have loose ball bearings. But if you ever wanted to roller skate, why not use them? Your hardest trouble will be most likely to find a roller rink with a wooden floor. If no luck, you could see if your sidewalk is flat, and made of cement to skate on. Or if you know of someone who has a barn out in the country with a wooden floor, you could try using them in the barn. Most likely, you might have to take them to a roller rink (or call first) to see if they would have the bearings and wheels to convert the old wooden wheels over to plastic wheels. You don't want to use the wooden wheels on a plastic coated floor, because the wooden wheels would tear up the plastic on the floor.

But, let's say that you found a location to roller skate with the wooden wheels. Here's how you would get these skates back in working condition: you will first need an old towel to work on a workbench, a 9/16-inch box-end wrench and socket with a screwdriver type handle; an 11/16 inch wrench (flat-skate wrench), a screwdriver to tighten your trunk adjustment bolts and toe stops. Page 38 shows the different parts of the roller skate.

You will also need lubrication, if the bearings are rusty. You will need transmission fluid for automatic transmissions, or WD-40, or lubricating oil, anything that breaks up rust and lubes, because, as you skate, that type of lubrication will help to remove the rust from the bearings.

After lubricating after about one to three hours of skating, it's a good idea to reclean and lubricate your wheels to remove rust that came off the bearings until they shine. I believe that after about four times of skating and cleaning, the rust should be off the ball bearings. If using transmission fluid, use something like an oil gun to put whatever drops you need in the ball bearings.

If your ball bearings are not rusty you may get any oil for lubrication, like motor oil (20, 10W30, any grade), lubricating oil or WD-40.

(1) Place an old towel on your workbench. This is because there are 16 loose ball bearings to each wheel. As you repair one wheel at a time, the bearings will not be rolling as far away from you when they are released from the wheel.

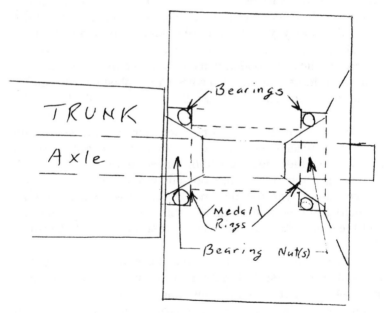

Figure 1

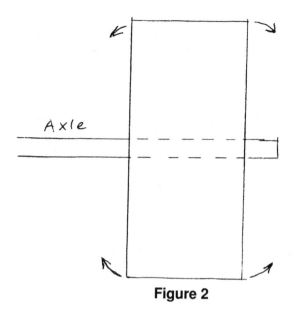

Axle

Figure 2

(2) About a 3/8 inch socket should remove the lock nut. Then remove the dust cover as seen on page 38. Then remove the washer. If you can't find the washer, it might be stuck on the back of the dust collector.

(3) Probably a 9/16 inch socket would be best in removing the outer bearing nut, but remember to be careful, because as you turn it counterclockwise to remove the outer bearing nut, you will have eight ball bearings rolling on your towel. Also, keep the wheel toward the skate, so that the eight inner bearings won't be rolling around also. Then slowly remove the wheel from the axle and let the eight inner ball bearings drop on the towel.

(4) Take a 9/16 inch box-end wrench and put a little pressure on the wrench to make sure that the inner bearing nut is tight.

(5) If bearings are rusty, make sure that all the ball bearings are off your outside and inside metal rings (Figure #1). Count your bearings. If you have fifteen bearings, eight go

41

in the inside part of the wheel. The last seven go on the outside. That's so that when you get to the rink, you should be able to buy whatever you need in the line of bearings. And add one bearing to it to complete your eight ball bearings on the outside of the skate wheel.

(6) Put the outside of the wheel, facing down on your towel. And put the axle of the skate in the wheel enough so that the eight ball bearings will not fall out of the bottom of the wheel. But put the skate high enough so that you can put your bearings in the inside half of the wheel. You might have to turn the wheel around some, so that the bearings will not be in a pile. When this is done, lift the wheel up, so that the ball bearings will be resting on the inner bearing nut and metal ring. When the wheel can't go any higher, turn the skate upside down so that that wheel will be up in the air.

(7) Now, place the rest of the bearings in the wheel, and turn the outer bearing nut that's going on the axle in a clockwise direction, until the nut is snug against the bearings. The nut should be loose enough for the wheel to spin.

(8) With rusted bearings, add about three drops of transmission fluid to the inner bearings and about three drops to the outer. Take a finger and spin the skate wheel. After a few spins, take the outer bearing nut off and take the ball bearings out of the wheel. And use another cloth to "pinch" each bearing to clean off the rust and transmission fluid. This should have taken some rust from the bearings, bearing nuts, and metal rings. Also, wipe off both bearing nuts. You can use your pinky finger with an old cloth, to clean the metal rings. Then disassemble, clean, assemble, and lubricate at least two more times.

(9) After spinning the skate wheel a few times, disassemble the wheel again. Take the 9/16 inch closed-end wrench to make sure the inner bearing nut is tight with small pressure for tightening. After installing the bearings, put the outer nut on. Add motor or lubricating oil, about two drops to the inner and two drops to the outer ball bearings. And spin the wheel so that it spins freely, but doesn't wiggle much as in Figure #2.

(10) When adjusted, add your washer and dust collector. The dust collector reduces the chance of dust getting into your ball bearings. Each particle of dust means that you have to work that much harder to roller skate. But sometimes, when you tighten your lock nut, the outer bearing nut will get out of adjustment, so spin the wheel to make sure that it's not too tight. Wiggle it to make sure it's not too loose. If the outer nut won't cooperate after several attempts for adjustments, take the dust collector off. And you might be able to use an open-end wrench to keep the outer bearing nut in the adjusted position while you tighten the lock nut.

If the bearings aren't rusty, take the bearings out of the wheel. Wipe out the metal rings. Wipe off the bearing nuts. And "pinch" each bearing between a cloth to clean them. Put the wheel back together and adjust the outer bearing nut. Then lock it with the lock nut. Also, lubricate and spin the wheel.

(11) Then go to another wheel. Do the same thing, until you're done.

(12) Use a large screwdriver to tighten the toe stops.

(13) Turn to page 32 on how to "adjust your trunks."

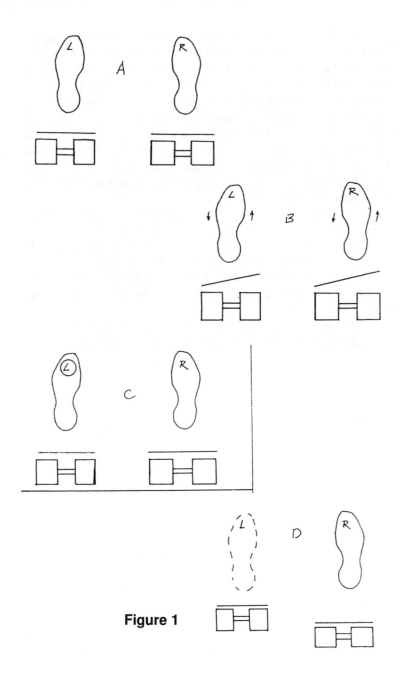

Figure 1

8

Skating Frontwards

This and the following chapters on skating are on how to interpret the feet and its codes. In Figure #1-A, it shows that your ankles (feet) have weight distribution on both feet. Then Figure #1-B shows that on both the left and right foot, you use your foot muscles to force down on the left side of each skate. You would most likely do this by coasting around a left corner. Figure 1-C shows that with the circle around the letter "L," you have most of your body weight on your left foot, much less weight on your right foot. And Figure #1-D shows that your left foot is off the floor with the broken line. This means that 100 percent of your body weight is now on your right foot.

Before skating, make sure that your shoelaces are tight. You should have a smaller blister on your feet at the end of the skating session. Stores also sell insoles that go in your skates, on the bottom of the shoe. Since I've been using them in my roller skates, I have not had a blister on my feet. Another advantage of having your own skates, is that you don't have to forget to take them out of rental skates and give the insoles to someone else.

When you skate, you will skate in a counterclockwise direction on the skate floor, unless instructed to do otherwise, like in a "Reverse Skate."

It makes no difference about the angle of your feet, as long as the feet are not pointed straight ahead. "Angle" means that if your heels are two inches apart, your toes should be one inch, or three inches or more apart. Your skates would be pointing ahead, if your toes and heels are about two inches apart. I have found out in my many years of skating, that you should try to

Beginner's Skate

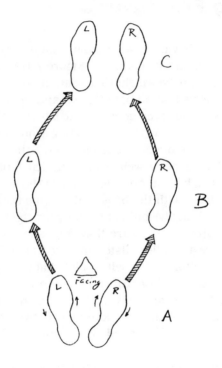

Figure 2

Beginner's Skate (corners)

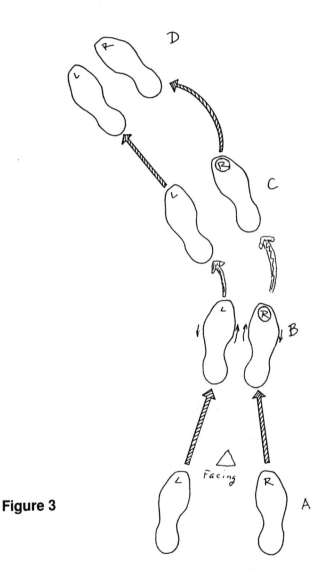

Figure 3

make the most of each angle while skating. And the faster you move your feet, the faster you go. The slower you move your feet, the slower you go. So you can regulate your own speed. Now, let's learn to skate.

First, try the Beginner's Skate on a skate floor, off from the main skating floor. Place your feet basically as in Figure #2-A, with your heels touching together, and about two inches apart at the toes. You then use your leg muscles to push your feet out. This will thrust you forward. You can extend both feet from one to six inches from their original distance apart as in Figure #2-B. Then use your muscles to bring your toes in and bring your skates together until the roller skates are about two to four inches from each other. Then you extend your feet, and continue doing this.

Now that you are either coming up to a wall or a hand rail, this how to make your left turn. In Figure #3-A, your feet are apart. In Figure #3-B, your skates come to about two inches apart. In Figure #3-C, you shift most of your body weight on your right foot and have less weight on your left foot. Force your left foot to move the toe of your skate to the left. This is shown in Figure #3-C. You then swing your right foot out and bring the right foot back again as in Figure #3-D. You continue this until you have made your left turn. When you are roller skating in a straight line, it would be a good idea to lift one of your skates at a time off the floor periodically. This will help you to learn how to control your balance on one foot, while skating.

Let's say that after a few trips around the floor, you have mastered the Beginner's Skate real good. Also you have a better balance on your skates by skating on either foot. Now you want to increase your knowledge about skating some more. The Vee Skate goes like this. After you use your toe stop(s) or the Beginner's Skate to get you moving, and your feet are together as in Figure #4-A, you put your body weight on your left foot and aim it straight ahead. Then extend your right foot to the right about six to twelve inches as in Figure #4-B. This will give

Vee Skate

Figure 4

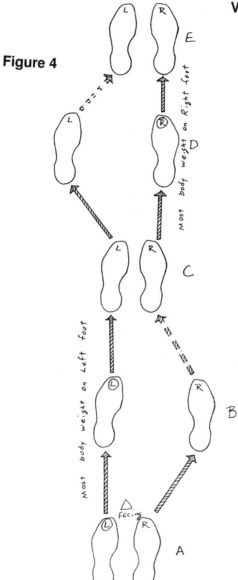

Vee Skate (corners)

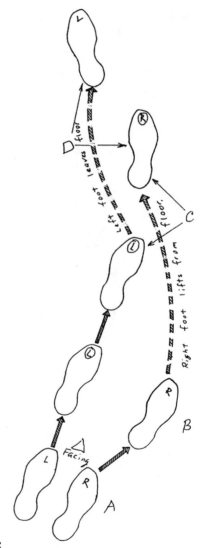

Figure 5

you a thrust forward, while your skates remain on the floor. With your weight on your left skate, you can now lift the right skate off the floor and bring it close to your left foot as in Figure #4-C.

You may now shift your weight to your right foot and push your left foot out, while the skate is still on the floor to give you drive forward as in Figure #4-D. After your left foot has been extended about six inches, lift it off the floor and place it next to your right foot as in Figure #4-E.

Before you know it, you're coming up to the wall again. So, with both feet on the floor as in Figure #5-A, you push out your right feet as before, but when you lift the right foot off the floor, you move it in front of your left skate and angle the foot to the left to continue your circle and place your right foot on the floor about two inches from your left foot as in Figure #5-B. In Figure #5-C, you shift your weight to the right foot and bring your left foot in back of your right and angle the left foot to the left, before placing it on the floor. *Remember,* that before you lift the right foot off the floor, push the right skate away from you by using your right leg muscles to keep your speed while either going around the corner or the straightaway.

As you skate more, you will be able to skate more smoothly and develop your own style of roller skating.

Now that you're moving right along, if you want to stop, all you have to do is to drag one of your skates behind you with the toe stop touching the floor. The more pressure that you put on the toe stop, the quicker you slow down. If you are going too fast, you could just sit down on the floor to help prevent you from running into someone; but get up and get going as soon as possible so that no one will run into *you.* People sometimes get hurt on skates, but by being careful and not going too fast, you can greatly reduce the risk of serious injuries.

Backwards Beginner's Skate

Figure 6

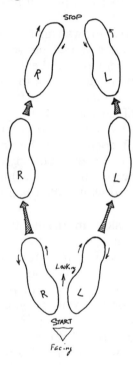

Figure 7

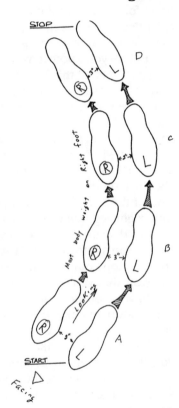

Backwards Beginner's Skate (curve)

9
Backwards Skating

You skate basically like the Beginner's Skate, except that you face the opposite direction that you want to go (or your back is heading in the direction of your skating). You start with the toes of your skates toward each other while your heels are about one or two inches farther apart as in Figure 6-A. When you extend your feet, this will cause you to go backwards. *Remember*: when you're skating backwards, look over either shoulder. Not only will you be able to see in the direction that you are going, but you'll be able to see better going around the corners at the rink.

Another advantage is that if someone cuts through the center of the rink's floor and comes toward you, you have a better chance of seeing them to brace yourself so that you might not fall. Your neck will get tired if you leave it in this position for a period of time, so the best time to look over the opposite shoulder is on the straightaway when you know it's safe, or when you want to leave the floor. Turn your head from side to side only when you are sure it is safe to do so. To skate backwards is just as easy as extending both of your feet and bringing them together again as in Figure 6, A–C.

When you come to your curve, make sure you are looking over your right shoulder while skating backwards. As your skates are together as in Figure 7-A, shift your body weight to your left foot and force the heel of your right skate just enough off the floor so that you can move it to your right (anywhere from 5° to 45°) as in frame B.

Continue to do this until you're around the turn. After you've mastered this, the faster you do this, the faster you go.

Figure 8, frame A shows the Backwards Half-Eight Skate. The skates are together and you are traveling backwards. You shift your body on your left foot while extending your right foot out about four inches and keeping both skates on the floor as in frame B. Frame C is when you bring your right foot next to your left. Now you shift your weight on your right foot and while leaving your left skate on the floor, you extend it as in frame D and then bring it back as in frame E. When you come to a curve, use the same procedure as you would in Figure 7.

The Backwards In-Line Skate will help you to control your balance when you have one skate in front of the other and will also be helpful when you start to skate sideways. Before starting this skate, it might be a good idea to bend your knees a little or else when you extend your feet, you'll feel your body going down and coming up when you bring them together. Plus you'll skate more comfortably. As your feet are in position of Figure 9-A, move your right foot to your back while letting your left foot move in the front of you just enough so that you bring both of your feet, one in front of the other as in frame B. Figure 9-C shows that you extend both feet about four inches (you make the final judgment, of course) and then bring them back in line of one another again. When you come to a curve, you may continue to skate the way you are, with only two differences: (1) You lean your body around the curve to your right (or toward the center of the rink). (2) Your left leg will be straight while your right will be bent some and your weight while skating is placed on the left foot.

When you fall, do you spread out like a "Six Weeks Washing" and dust mop the floor with your back, plus end up at the bottom of a "Jam Pile:" In gym, you might have been taught the reverse roll. You can use this same basic roll on skates. But be sure to try it a few times without skates to get the feel of it first. I thought of this when I first started roller skating at the roller rink in Mount Morris, Michigan, around

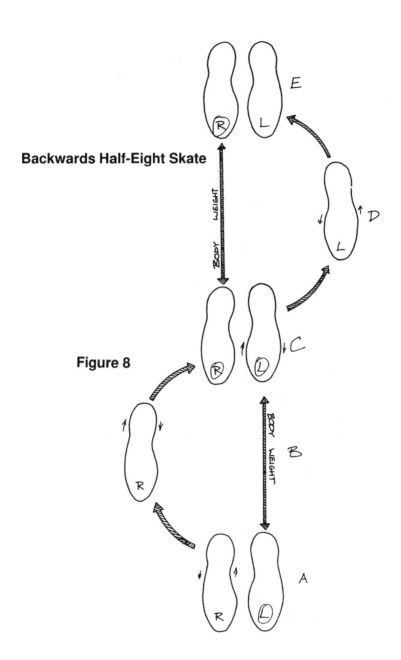

Backwards Half-Eight Skate

Figure 8

Backwards In-line Skate

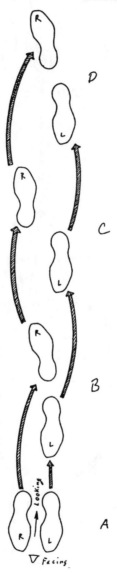

Figure 9

1966. In Figure 10, frame A, you are skating backwards and you had just lost your balance or someone hit you, which caused you to lose your balance. You might as well admit to yourself that you are going to fall and go along with it. It's best to practice this on skates where there are very few people and at a distance away from others so that when you do fall, others will have plenty of time to skate around you. Or try this in the middle of the floor.

In Frame B, you are falling to the floor. When you hit the floor as in Figure 10-C, lean back and kick your feet over your head while arching your back so that you can roll like a ball as in Frame D. *Remember* to keep your arms alongside of you so that no one will run over them. Also keep your feet about four inches apart and parallel of each other.

In Frame D, you will notice that the back of his head is touching the floor as much as possible. It's important to use this part of the head so that you will greatly reduce your chances of having a "headache." By practicing this beforehand, you will know how far you can move your feet around over your head, while the back of your head is on the floor. Now use your hands to lift your head up off the floor so that your skates will settle on the floor. Also remember to keep your feet parallel to each other at all times, so that you will be able to get back up on your skates much easier as in Frame F.

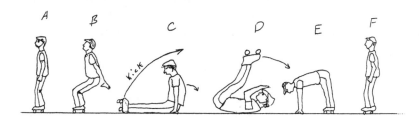

Figure 10

57

I hope that you don't have a night like I did around 1978 when I was skating at Edra Roller Rink in Holt, Michigan. I was skating and doing my regular thing when I hit something on the floor that caused me to lose my balance. I didn't think too much of it because I've fallen before many times going backwards and it looked like this was going to be an "Instant Replay." So, down I went. Put when I got up, down I went again. I thought, *Man, what's going on around here. I have done this a million times and stayed up on my feet. I'll try it one more time.* So I went through that ceremony again. And you know what? I went down the second time! I thought that that was the last straw. *I'm going to stop being a tumbleweed and get up like a man who has just fallen. And skate with my skates, and let the wheels do the rolling instead of me. If I keep this up, I'd better gain some weight to see if I can roll any better* (ha-ha).

Just a few months after this happened, around 1979 I had another experience with my "Big Brain Idea." If you have taken science, you will know that when an airplane drops a bomb, the bomb doesn't go straight down, but as it falls, it remains going forward because of its being under motion before its release. That's the same way in skating, when you skate and lose your balance and begin to fall. You are still moving in that same direction, except for this one time.

When I lost my balance at this particular church skating party, I felt like I was shot out of a cannon on wheels. That is, the cannon moved, which left me hanging in mid-air, until the gravity took a good hold of me and brought me down to earth. I was so "stunned" by the experience that I couldn't sit down for at least five minutes. I hurt so much of where I sit down that it felt like my dad had just given me a spanking. And I'm trying to figure out what I had done wrong! With skates, you sure have your ups and downs!

Besides this, a pole about twenty-four inches in diameter at Durand Rink and I connected one time. Larry Prior, Becky Doyle (at that time), and I were skating in a Trio Skate. We were skating about three-fourths my speed (someone like me traveling that fast should have their head examined) and were going around a curve at the rink (with me on one of the ends). Then all of a sudden, this pole came charging right at me. I didn't have time to think to myself that, *There's a pole coming right at me.* I had time to think of only maybe the first three words, and that was it. I didn't know if I was going to crack up like in the cartoons, or the pole. But if it was going to be me, I didn't want to get any blood on the floor, so I hurried into the men's room. That was the only time that I've ever gotten a fat lip from running into a pole on skates, but after thinking about it, I have fewer accidents on skates than I do being on the road. Maybe I'm telling myself that it would be better for everyone if I handed in my driver's license.

In Figure 11, we have the Forwards-to-Backwards. Now after skating backwards and you get the fundamentals well enough so that you can do it without much fear of falling, let's try to skate forwards and turn around and skate backwards. It's easier to practice this while going around a curve, but if you have too much fear of falling down, then try this on the straightaway. In Figure 11, frame A, you shift your body weight on your right foot. Frame B is when you lift your left skate just off the floor. You bring your left skate in behind your right skate while rotating your body counterclockwise as in frame C. In frame D, you place your left skate in back of your right with the heels of both skates facing each other. And then place the left foot on the skate floor. Shift your body weight to your left skate and lift your right foot as in frame E. Frame F shows the completed rotation of your right skate so that you are skating backwards now. When your skates are parallel, put your right foot on the floor and shift your weight to both skates.

Do this again; go from backwards skating to skating frontwards.

You might fail a few times, but by continual practice and trying different ways to skate, in time, you will be skating as if there's nothing to it. But it does take time and practice.

Skating Forwards to Backwards

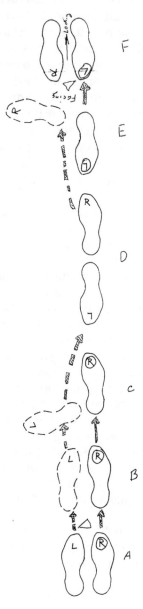

Figure 11

Skating Backwards to Forwards (curve)

Figure 12

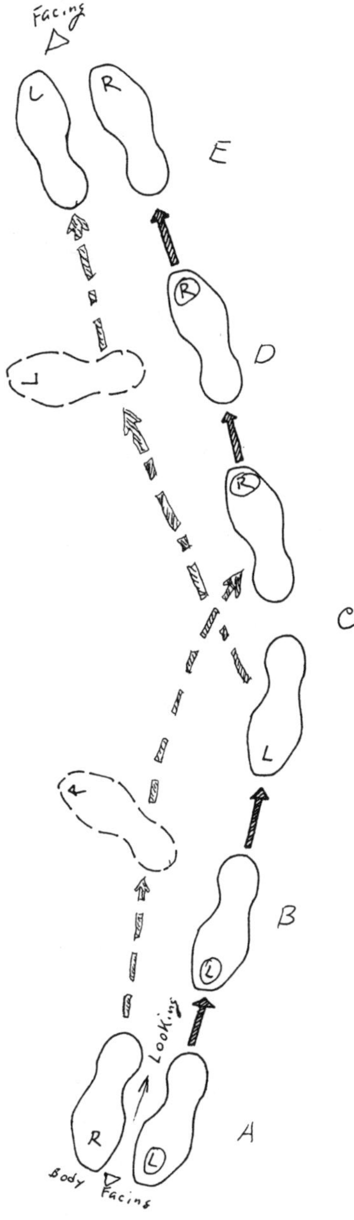

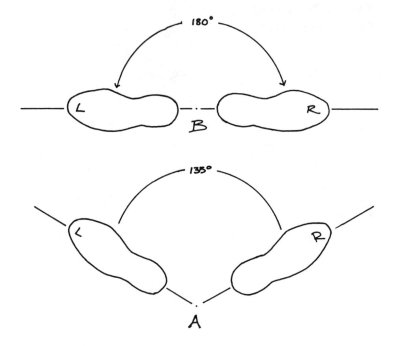

Figure 13

10
Skating Sideways

Suppose you are coming up to two people who are moving slower than you are. And you cannot go around them, plus, you want to retain your speed. If the two people are about two feet apart, this is where skating sideways comes in handy.

I believe that it's easier to start skating sideways around a curve because your feet are not at a 180 angle, but more of an 135 angle. To illustrate my point, place your feet (without skates on) in the position of Figure 13, frame A. Your feet don't have to be exactly 135 . Just place them approximately at that angle. Now, place your feet as in Figure 13-B in a 180 angle. If you are not used to putting your feet this position, you find out that it's hard to stand up. But when you're under motion on skates, it's much easier to keep your balance. If you fall while trying to skate sideways, try different speeds, angles of your feet, or try this on the straightaway. Each person is different and will have to try different approaches when it comes to skating around the corners.

At Figure 14, frame A, we have both skates on the floor and your body weight is on both feet. Now, you shift your weight on your right foot and lift your left foot off the skating floor.

Bring your foot around in back of you as in frames B and C. You might try leaning to the center of the rink when turning a corner to see if this will give you better control of your skates. When you come to frame D, then you can place your left foot on the floor. If you fall, do not shift your weight immediately to both feet, but place it just touching the floor so that if you lose control of your skate again, you can raise the left foot before it trips you because of your body weight still being on your right foot. When after a few feet with your left foot just touching the floor and if it doesn't feel like it's going to cause you to fall, then you can shift your weight to both skates. Try this around the corners first several times before doing anything fancy.

Skating Frontwards to Sideways (curve)

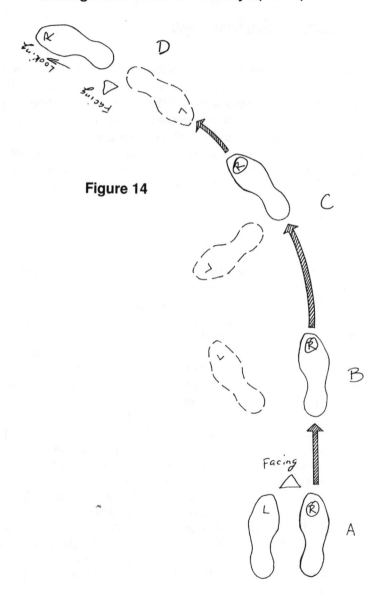

Figure 14

Skating Sideways to Frontwards

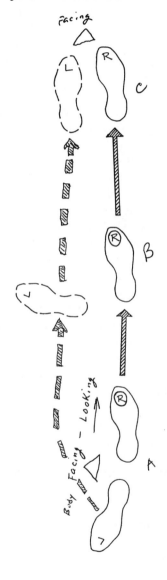

Figure 15

To skate from sideways to frontwards as in Figure 15, at frame A, shift your body weight to your right foot and lift your left foot off the floor. Bring your left foot from behind your right toward the front as in frame B. When your left foot is in the position of 15-C (side-by-side), place it on the floor and shift your weight to both feet. When you do, this is when your right foot is pointed in the direction that you want to go. As you continue to skate sideways around a curve, experience will help in determining how much to lean. Leaning will depend upon two factors: 1) how fast you're going, and 2) the size of the circle that you want to make.

When an airplane makes a turn in the air, you will notice that the wings tilt. If the plane makes a left turn, the left wing is dropped closer to the ground, when compared to the right. And so it is with roller skating. When you come to the turn in the rink, you can move more easily around the curve if you lean toward the center of the rink a little until you complete your circle. Also, you can control your turn by using your toe stops. As you're moving sideways, if you move your toes toward the 180 angle, you lengthen your turn. If you move your toes toward each other, like the 135 angle, you shorten your circle.

Figure 16 shows us that you're going backwards and you want to go sideways around an oncoming corner. Frame A is where you shift your body weight to your left skate and raise your right foot off the floor. As you bring your right foot around to position of frame B, you also turn your body with it as well as the other sideways skating. Frame C is a position in which you can fall easily if you are not careful. This is because you are going in a straight line and all of a sudden, your right foot is headed in a different direction. To reduce your chances of "wiping out" (falling), just before you place your right foot on the floor, move your left toe toward the center of the rink some so that you start your circle. You can then place your right foot on the floor to continue the turn. You can then place your body weight on both skates.

Backwards to Sideways

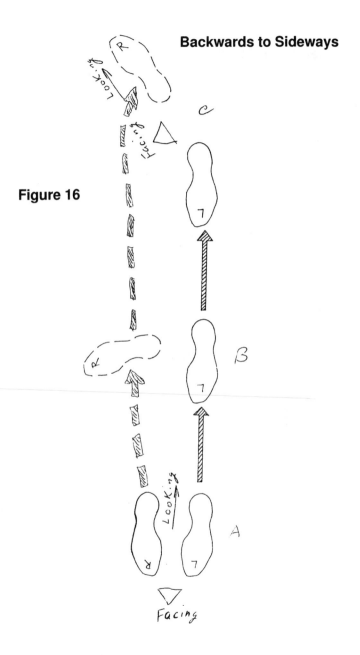

Figure 16

Sideways to Backwards

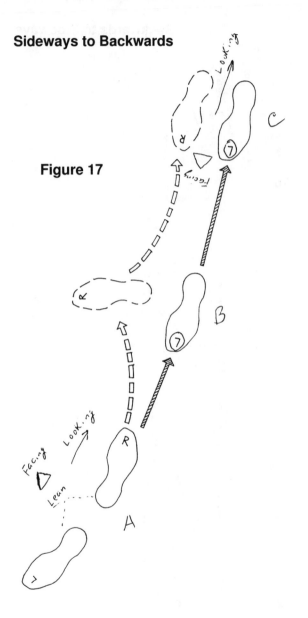

Figure 17

Now, let's suppose that you've made your turn and you're coming to the straightaway. Figure 17 shows us how to skate from sideways to backwards. In frame A, shift your body weight to your left foot. Lift up your right foot off the floor. As you turn to have your back going in the direction that you are going, bring your right skate with you and go from frame B to frame C. You will then place your right foot on the floor of the rink and will be traveling backwards. *Remember* to place your chin on your right shoulder when you're in the center of the rink. This is so that you can see in back of you and dodge someone if they should fall. When you're on the outside of the rink, look over your left shoulder to see if someone will go on the floor without looking. If someone does, you will be able to stop, but when you come to the corner, look over your right shoulder.

You can, after a while, try to skate sideways on the straightaway. In time, you will be able to skate sideways all around the skating rink floor. Now we'll come to the part of keeping you moving while you're skating sideways as in Figure 18. You can experiment first from changing your body weight on both feet, then having most of your weight on your right foot. I put about two-thirds of my weight on my right foot and the other third on my left foot. This weight on the left skate will reduce the chances of the skate from sliding to give you the power that you need to keep going. Most of your weight on the right foot will help you to continue the direction that you want to go with little interference from the left skate. As Figure 18 shows, as you're going sideways, just move your left foot back and forth from your right foot as in frames A, B, and C.

In going around the curves, as you can see in Figure 19, the left foot goes behind the right, as in frame A, extended toward the center of the floor for push, as in frame B. Frame C shows us that we then place the skate behind the right again to continue the push. It's easier to skate this way on the corners, when you don't extend the left foot beyond (or outside) of the right.

Side Skate Push

Figure 18

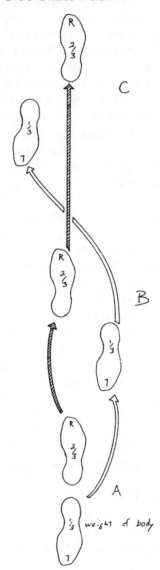

Skating Sideways (curve)

Figure 19

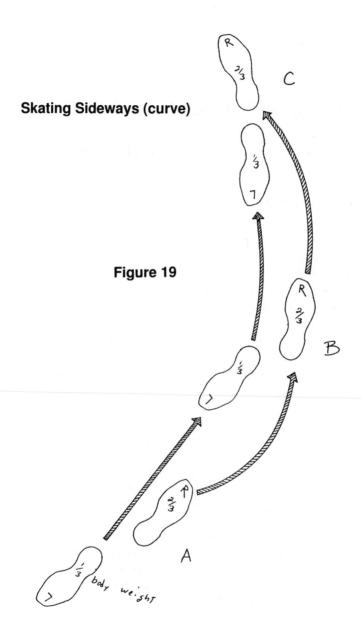

11

Ten Suggestions at the Rink

There are ten suggestions that you should know and apply at each skating rink.

1. Go to have fun.
2. Be courteous.
3. Be friendly.
4. No speed skating.
5. No racing.
6. Look where you're going.
7. Don't weave on the skate floor.
8. Always wear socks (if renting skates).
9. Throw unwanted trash in proper containers, not on the floors.
10. No refreshments and gum outside of the refreshment stand.

1. Go to Have Fun

Recreation is a time of fun. This is what we (the owners of the rinks and I) want everyone to do. But there are some who cannot put away arguments from school, work, or home. It's hard, I know, to keep still when someone is there whom you dislike. But each person should go skating to have fun, not to fight. Why spoil someone else's evening or afternoon just to get even! If you dislike someone, please leave them alone. They might be going through some problems that you might not even know of. If you say something, say something nice. Try to translate what the other person had said as meaning something good. Try also to let the negative part go in one ear and faster out the other. *Remember*, only you and the other person can start a fight or use bad language at one another. Either you might start an argument or the other person might. You or the other person could have done something to start the argument. If the argument develops into a fight, then the both of you are guilty. The two of you could be asked to leave the rink and if it is not stopped, both of you will not be able to return to the rink and will be classified as "trouble makers." It's not worth it. So go to have fun and do the best you can to stay out of fights and arguments.

2. Be Courteous

Have you ever been courteous to others? Many times when I've been skating, someone comes along, and bumps me. They usually continue on their way, but sometimes they will excuse themselves. The ones who "excuse" themselves are being courteous. Whether it's my fault or not, if the other person doesn't excuse themselves after a few seconds, I do. Even if it isn't my fault, I try to say, "Excuse me."

I can remember skating about two hours at a skating rink. I was going backwards and this one guy went around a curve and came out in back of me. When we were about three feet apart, he stopped. It startled me so much that I ran right into him. My first thoughts were: *You stupid idiot. You saw me coming and you just wanted me to run into you.* But I said to him, "Oh, excuse me." He smiled and said, "That's OK!" He might have been looking for a fight. Or he might have just want me to say something. But then, he might have just wanted to test me to see what I would do. If you want someone to talk to you, the best thing to do is to go to that person and talk to them.

"Couples Only" skate is a good time. That's why the DJ

should announce "Ladies Choice" at a skating session to give the girls a chance to ask a boy to skate since the guys usually ask the girls.

What I have just said is nothing new. My Lord Jesus spoke of this in Matthew 7:12, " . . . whatsoever ye would that men should do to you, do ye even so to them . . . " In other words, if you don't want someone to give you a black eye, don't give others a black eye. If you don't want someone to steal your thousand-dollar stereo, don't steal someone else's stereo. Whatever you want others to do to you, you do it to them. And if you believe that you have the right to steal, then you're one person that I want to stay away from.

3. Be Friendly

We all need friends nowadays, not enemies. We need to talk to someone about our problems, fears, etc. By being friendly and not telling others what someone else has said and keeping it to yourself, we can increase our friends and communicate better with others and do our part to help this world to become a better place in which to live. Only when this world becomes better, will a girl be able to ask a guy for a ride home if she needs one. Because today, anything could happen to her. So it's a job for each one of us to make this a better and safer world.

4. No Speed Skating

If you are caught speeding in a car, you will get a ticket. If you get too many tickets, you will lose your driver's license. That's basically what happens when you are caught speeding in a rink. First, you are asked to "slow down." Then you will usually have to sit down for a few minutes. If this doesn't work, then you will lose your right to roller skate because you were abusing your freedom of skating.

A speeding skater is one who is skating much faster than others. Each rink has an idea of how much faster you can go before the floor manager will ask you to "slow down." That's one of the main job of theirs, to control the speeders. You've heard about the "innocent always getting hurt." That's about the way it is on skates also. When a fast skater and an innocent person collide together, the person not at fault usually gets hurt. What you do at the rink could change their policy also!

To prove my point. I went to a roller rink and I started to skate backwards. The floor manager asked me to turn around because backward skating was not allowed unless it was for "Backward Skating Only." I found out later on that someone was skating backwards and was not watching where they were going, so they bumped into someone, which caused serious injury to the other person. That person sued the roller rink. To reduce the chances of someone getting hurt and getting sued again, the owners changed the policy to no backwards skating unless on a special skate for backwards skaters. This has nothing to do with the speeders, but in time it could. So, fellas, slow down, please. I have seen the time when one night at a rink, the girls had two songs to skate to. But the guys didn't have even half a song when the DJ said "All Skate" because the guys were skating too fast.

5. No Racing

Racing is when you're trying to go faster than one or more other guys. This is even more dangerous than the speed skater. The speed skater is one person and can hurt one, maybe two people. But in racing, you have two or more people trying to outdo the others. Which makes racing much more dangerous. Fellas, if you want to race, ask the manager to have a Race

Special Skate." Usually they will have the girls up to 13 years of age race first. Then girls from 14 to 17. Finally, girls over 18 will race. The guys will come next with the same age levels in each race as did the girls. The first group of up to 13 years of age should go around the floor just one time to determine the winner. The group from 14 to 17 can go two laps around the rink. From 18 and up, they can go two or three laps.

6. Look Where You're Going

If you're skating frontwards, not only do you look where you're going, but you should also pay attention to both sides of you. You don't know when someone will cut through the center of the floor or come out onto the skate floor. As in driving a car, you are watching for other cars or small kids running out from between parked cars so that you can stop quick enough to prevent someone from getting hurt or killed. So also be on the watch for those who are not alert so that the two of you and others are not hurt.

When you're skating backwards, always have your partner looking for the unexpected. If you're skating with someone and they are going backwards, if somebody falls, you can steer your friend to one side with your hands, away from the fallen person. Watching out for everyone is not just the other person's responsibility. It's everyone's responsibility.

When I skate, I try to leave about three or four feet between the wall (or rail) and myself. This is so that if the inexperienced skater wants to skate on the floor (or anyone), they will have the room to go on the floor. The more experienced you become on skates, the more you should be watching out for the other person. This is because the experienced person can control his or her skates much better than the inexperienced.

7. Don't Weave on the Skate Floor

The figure to your right illustrates some one weaving in a rink. This person is not going in a straight line but is going too

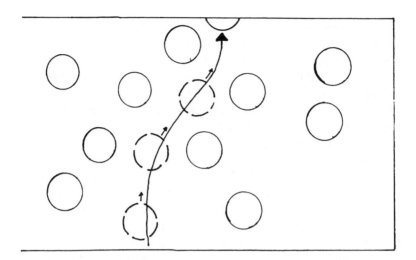

fast and is ducking around others. This is dangerous because if he sees a good place to go between two people up ahead, by the time he arrives in back of them, they might not have noticed him and he could have gotten a little closer without them knowing it. When he goes to cut between the two, something could happen that would cause the three to fall on the skate floor, plus, those who were too close to stop. They could fall or maybe have their fingers run over by others to cause injury.

It's like a reel of moving pictures. Each picture on the reel shows parts of a movie. It might show, for example on a frame, a man walking with his right heel about one foot from the sidewalk that he is walking on. On the next frame, the foot might have dropped two inches. What happens if someone broke a glass just before he stepped down on the sidewalk? He could be seriously hurt. But if the reel was in a projector, then it looks more real. The movement is smoother and you can judge much better what is going on if the camera is far enough away.

One time I was skating at a small roller rink when they had just one light shining toward the floor. It flashed the light on and off. I didn't like it because it was hard for me to judge what the others were going to do. My fear was so great that I slowed down. In one flash of the light, a person could be far enough away so that I wouldn't have to worry about a collision. But in the next flash of the light, I might. That's like what could happen between two frames on the reel of pictures. It might be OK for those who are used to it, but I didn't like it. Each one who skates should know their limit and try to use common sense. This will help to reduce the unknown surprises of running into someone.

If someone near the center of the floor decides that they want to get off the floor, many times they will cut through the floor and usually get bumped into a lot before getting off. If you want to get off the floor, be sure to work your way to the outside of the floor. Then, when you come to your exit, please do not cut through the skaters who are skating on the floor. You could knock others down. As a driver looks before he makes a lane change, so must the skater look also. So be sure to look behind you to see if someone is coming up fast in the direction that you are traveling.

Another way of dangerous weaving is skating against the roller skaters. I can remember a few years back one disco song, it had a few parts where an instrument had a low pitch and would gradually obtain a high pitch. This one person would show others how to time it so that he and his friends would prepare themselves at the low pitch. They would cut through the skaters so that they would "do their thing" in front of the disc jockey's desk at the high pitch. I hope that each one of you uses more sense than this. Yes, they were having fun, but at the risk of injury to themselves and others?

8. Always Wear Socks

When I joined the Air Force a few years back, my training instructor told us to always wear our shower clogs whenever we took a shower so that we would reduce the chances of getting athlete's foot. This applies to those who rent their skates. Each foot does have bacteria, but some bacteria is not good for your feet. By wearing socks, you might prevent yourself from getting bad bacteria or spreading it to someone else. I know of a lady who skated without socks. She had her own skates, but no one else used them, except her. Even if you buy a used pair of skates or new, use socks for your feet's health.

Also, the sock is used as a cushion between your feet and the skate. Pull some on the shoelaces when putting skates on to reduce the chances of your feet and skates rubbing together to cause a blister. After skating about one hour, when it's time to "clear the floor" for the next skate special, pull on the laces from the bottom of the skate, and work your way to the top of the shoe. If you have slack in your shoelace, then you can tighten it, but don't pull so hard on your laces that you will cut off your circulation to your feet. Time will instruct you as to how tight to have them pulled.

9. Throw Unwanted Trash in Containers

The roller rink should be a safe place to skate, instead of a hazardous place. Yet, skating becomes a hazard when anyone throws or drops anything on the floor in the building. Even a small piece of paper could cause a skate to suddenly stop and send someone falling on a hard floor. When I skate I try to pick up anything that's on the floor. But sometimes there are many objects on the skating surface. What the floor needs then is a good dust mopping the next day. So if *you* want skating to be more safe, throw your unwanted trash in the trash container before continuing your skating.

Another way that roller rinks can be more safe is to have the managers or someone to check the skates over. After cleaning and adjusting my skates, I have found out that the lock nut sometimes comes loose after the first or second time I've used them. Trunks and toe stops come off rental skates often. Inspect the skate after cleaning and adjusting for the first and second skating session. Look for loose or tight wheels, loose or tight trunk and toe stops. Inspection could then be about once a month. This takes time, I know, but it's worth it if it will help prevent someone going to a hospital because of a wheel coming off, or a trunk. The owners have the right to think of profits, or safety first, but it's your decision if you want to have a safe night of skating, because not very many people will think of your safety.

10. No Refreshments or Gum Outside the Refreshment Area

When you stop skating for refreshments, consume what you buy. Then throw the cups, paper, etc., in the trash container before leaving the refreshment area. And then go skating.

Gum is also important to leave in the trash container. If you are bumped, you could open your mouth and it might fly out. Gum is sticky and could cause someone to fall and get hurt. Mothers might even get mad in trying to get it out of your clothing when washing. So please, throw the gum in the wastebasket before going on the skating surface. Just think, you can get a fresh stick when you're outside the skate building.

12

Skate Specials

After about four records of "All Skate" where everyone can skate, the rink manager or disc jockey can have a skate special. These skate specials can be used either for individuals to be given a chance to get to know one another more. Or, they can be used in competing with one another. There are skate specials like the tango, the two-step, etc. These specials can be given in a rink for those who take these special classes, but I refer to skate specials as couples, trio, race, and Grand March.

Couples Only

(1) COUPLES ONLY. This is where the guys usually ask the girls to skate. Because the guys ask the girls to go out on a date, it is also fitting that the boys should ask the girls to roller skate. In this skate, the couple would skate in the normal direction around the rink (counterclockwise) with the girl to his right (on the outside by the hand railing or wall). The boy and girl can skate forwards or backwards, whatever they like. If too many accidents happen while others are skating backwards, the manager could have everyone skating forwards. If a girl sees a guy who's just sitting around and not having much fun, I don't see why she can't go and ask him to skate with her. The most he can do is say "No." As for me, I'm used to that.

Two records should be played for these skating specials.

(2) LADIES CHOICE. This is where the girls ask the boys to skate. The girl is again to the fella's right.

(3) ADVANCED COUPLES. This is where couples are also

skating. At the sound of a whistle, the dong of a bell, music stops for about two seconds, etc. The guy "advances" to the girl in front of him. In this skate, the skaters skate with someone different so that they can get to know more than just one person. My suggestion here is to have each guy advance every forty-five seconds. This will give each couple a little time to talk. Before the gentleman goes on to the next girl, I would suggest in playing two records.

(4) SNOWBALL. This is a skate that starts with couples skating in the regular direction. Then at the word "Snowball" or blowing of a whistle over the PA system, the couples reverse direction. It's a lot of fun, but be very careful when turning around to go in the other direction so that no one will get hurt. The whistle could be blown every half minute for skaters to turn around. On the second and last record, when the record is about two-thirds done, the whistle could be blown every fifteen seconds apart, then ten and then every five seconds apart to add more fun to this special. And again, skaters, BE CAREFUL.

(5) LAST SKATE. This is to allow those who can find someone to skate with them, to skate. For those who cannot find someone to roller skate with, they can take their skates off and hand them in so that you don't have everyone in line after skating to hand in their skates.

Also "Reverse Skate" could be used.

Trio

(1) TRIO. This skate could have two girls at each side of the guy. Or one girl between two guys. You could also have three girls skating as well. If there happens to be an unskilled skater, it would be best to have that person between the two better skaters.

(2) CONGO. In a trio, the second song could be the Congo. You can have the three people get in a line to "kick." You have

a leader to lead the other two. The person in back of the leader places their hands on the waist of the leader. The third person places their hands on the person who's following the leader. On a given signal on the record, each person who's following their leader should watch to see which foot will be used to "kick" first. When you bring your feet to the floor, you will push yourself to keep moving. *Remember,* each time that you kick, you kick with a different foot each time; kick with left foot, skate with right and left foot, kick with right foot, skate with left and right foot, kick with left foot.

When I led, I liked skating backwards, because I was facing the opposite direction. We would still kick with the same foot so the person behind me and I would not kick each other. After the song, then it's an "All Skate."

(3) CRAZY TRIO. At the sound of the whistle, the three skaters in a group reverse direction. You should have at least one girl in each trio.

(4) ADVANCED TRIO. This skate usually has two girls and one boy, but if your group of skaters has more boys than girls, then have two guys and one girl. Whichever one you use, have all groups the same. At the sound of the whistle, the gentlemen will move forward.

Backwards Skating Only

All skaters in this skating special must skate in the regular direction, but skating backwards as described in the chapter of this book on "Backwards Skating." If you skate with someone, one person can skate backwards while the other is skating forwards.

Reverse Skating Only

At some roller rinks, after the "Backwards Skating Only,"

they have "Reverse Skating in Opposite Direction Only." This is an "All Skate," but the people skate in the opposite direction (clockwise) around the floor and skating backwards. After that song, you can have the skaters come to a complete stop, then have them skate in the normal direction.

Multiplication Skate

On this skate, you have the boys line up on the opposite side of the rink. The girls line up on the opposite side of the guys along the railing. Have one couple start out skating together. After about twenty seconds, blow the whistle for the guy to go to the girls' line and pick a girl. The girl goes to the guys' line to pick a guy. Each person who is skating on the floor, goes to get someone of the opposite sex at each signal. When the skaters will not get a partner from the line, have the remaining go to the center of the rink. The floor manager should take a flashlight with him. If you have a girl, have her pick out a guy whom she wants to skate with. The girl who lost the guy, she goes to the back of the line. The boy slows down to let his new partner catch up. If a boy is next in line, he will pick a girl to skate with. If a boy or girl doesn't know who to skate with, just pick someone for them by shining the light on a couple.

Up and Down Skate

As everyone is skating to the "All Skate," inform them that the next record is the "Up and Down Skate." While the song is being played, when you give the signal (whistle), everyone will stoop down for about fifteen seconds. Give the signal again for everyone to stand up. Wait for about half a minute to blow the whistle again for them to stoop down again. This is good exercise and lots of fun to do.

Races

(1) RACES. This is the ordinary race as described on page 75 of this book under the heading of "No Racing."

(2) SCOOTER SKATE. In this race, the lead boy or girl could have one foot out in front of them, or have both skates on the floor together. I prefer having both skates together and on the floor because the lead person with the number one skate (Figure 20) can better dodge those who have fallen and retain their balance much easier as well. With one foot out, you are allowing the better skaters a chance of winning because the less skilled can fall easier. This prevents the pusher (skater number two in Figure 20) from not pushing as fast to cause their partner to fall. But the manager can decide which method to use.

(3) LOCOMOTIVE RACE. If you come up with a better name for this race, use it, but what this race basically consists of is that the leader (Figure 21), with skate number one) has his/her skates on the floor to steer the team around the curves, while his hands are on the skates of the person in back of him, who has number two skates. He should have his bottom as close to the floor as possible to bring his knees back so that the number two skater can reach over him (her) to place their two hands on the two knees of number one skater. All that skater number three does, is just push. Start pushing with both hands, then when coming to the corners, push with just one hand after that so that if the two people are "weaving," you can reduce your weaving. If they weave to your right, use your right hand to push on their back. If they weave to your left, use your left hand for pushing. The people in the figures show them wearing hats. But please, leave your hats at home. If the hat falls on the floor, someone might get hurt from tripping over it.

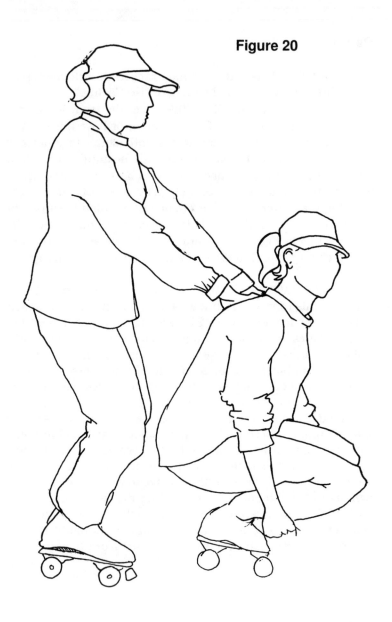

Figure 20

Figure 21

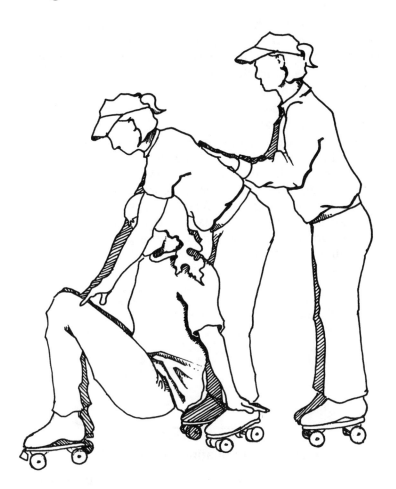

Grand March

The Grand March consists of starting out with couples in a long line. The girl is to the boy's right side again. The boy usually asks the girl, but the girl can ask if the guy is bashful. If the line is too long, the floor manager leads the group. He could have the couples line up against a wall or hand railing, but this skate special usually starts with the line in the middle of the floor (Figure 22).

Floor manager should clarify what the skaters who are close to him should do so that they will know what to do to have more fun. The other skaters follow the floor manager. In Figure 22, the "Floor Manager" is represented by a triangle. The blocks are the "Boys." The circles are the "Girls." When the music starts, the floor manager will motion for the couples to follow him. He can make simple skating procedures that are also outlined (Figure 22).

Figure 22

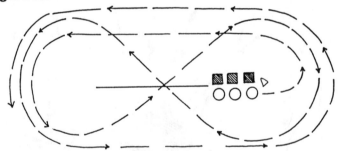

Each Couple Skating Side by Side

After you have finished this basic diagram, the manager can instruct the couples to get into a single line and have each couple pass the word to the back of the line. If the ones in back pay attention to the ones in front, they will know what to do before they are to do it. As the manager goes around the corner, stay with him close to the wall. About halfway, start to circle around to the other side of the floor. Continue on around and as you make each revolution on the floor, make it smaller each time (Figure 23).

Figure 23

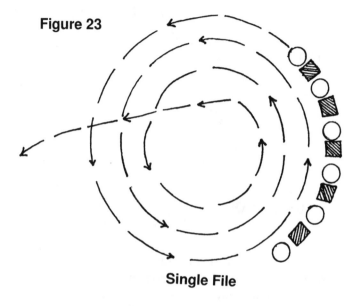

Single File

When you have nearly no room in the center, the manager tries to go outside the circles by going between two couples in the circle to reduce the chances of people running into each other. Try to keep in mind that once you reach the inside of the circle, you will be working your way out. When a couple goes past you who are still going in the circle, you and your partner will then cut between the couple going in the circle. After the two of you go by, then another couple goes by who are still going in the circle.

After everyone is out of the circle and still skating in single file, have them hold hands to form a large circle. The FM (Floor Manager) will take hold of the girl following him. She holds the hand of her skating partner. With his other hand, he holds the hand of the girl (lady) in back of him. All the other couples will do the same. When the FM holds the hand of the last guy, everyone will extend their arms out as far as possible to form a large circle (Figure 24).

Figure 24

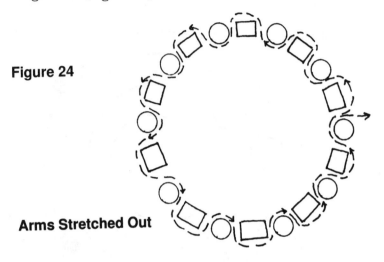

Arms Stretched Out

The FM will let go of the guy's hand and lead the one following him, in and out of the circle, underneath the arms of the skaters who are standing still. The standing skaters can help out by raising their hands as high as possible when the other skaters come to them. This really helps out when a tall person goes underneath the hands of smaller people. If you can skate well enough, you could put your head between your knees to allow yourself to become even lower yet.

After you have gone around the last person, go slow enough to allow the others to catch up when they are finished. After making a corner or two in single file, cut through the center of the floor and have the girls go one way, and the boys go another way in single file (Figure 25). At the opposite end of the rink, have the guys go on the outside of the floor and the girls on the inside. Then when they come close to the opposite side of the floor, have the girls go on the outside and the boys on the inside (opposite of the first passing). When the two lines come together the next time, have the first boy and girl come together and others who are following them and skate through the middle of the floor together again. You should now be well into the second record after skating around to give everyone a chance to become "reunited."

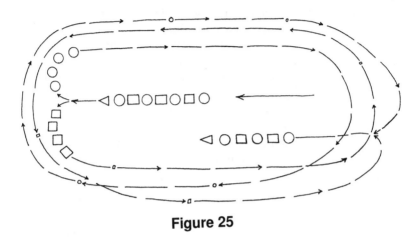

Figure 25

Cut through the center of the floor (Figure 26). Have couple number one go in one direction, the second couple in the opposite direction. The third couple will follow couple number one and pair number four will follow number two couple, etc.

Figure 26

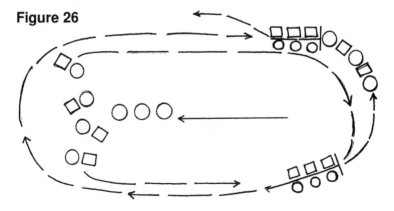

After the couples are divided into two lines, instruct one line to slow down. The other line gets into a long straight line and stops. Have those who stop to get as far away from their partner as possible, and raise their hands together as high as possible, girls on one side and the boys on the other. This forms a "bridge" for the other skaters. The FM leads the other skaters through the line in single file. He then takes them to the other side of the rink and has them stop to form a "bridge" for the opposite line after the second passing.

After making a circle around the rink, the two lines come to about the same distance from the corner to make their circle. They are then instructed by the FM as they come around the circle for the first couple in each line, to come together to form a single line of four people. The second couple in each of the two lines form a single line also through the center of the floor, etc. (Figure 27).

Figure 27

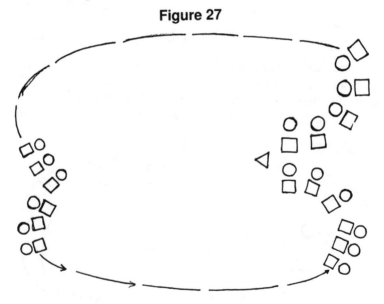

92

The best way to skate with four and more, in the Grand March, is illustrated in Figure 28. If each person is about the same height, it makes no difference whose arms are on the outside (to the front of the arms of the other person's) or inside. It's best for a tall person to have their hands at the outside so that he won't have to stoop down to get his/her arms underneath the shorter person. The shorter person feels more comfortable with his arms behind the taller person, so that the shorter person doesn't feel like they are being held up by the taller.

Figure 28

After skating around the floor of the rink, have them again cut through the rink's floor and have the first group go one way and the second group of four to go the other way. When they come toward each other at the opposite end of the rink, have the first group of both lines come together (Figure 29). When the FM sees that he has about twelve lines, he should be able to have an idea if he can make it into six lines for the "Wheel" in order for it to fit on the rink's floor, or remain as about twelve lines and have two "wheels." Let's say that there are seven lines with eight couples. Use the first six lines for the "spokes" of the "wheel." The couples in the seventh line can break off in pairs and attach themselves to one of the other lines.

Figure 29

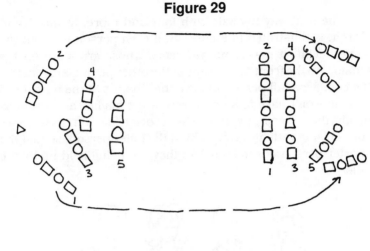

Figure 30

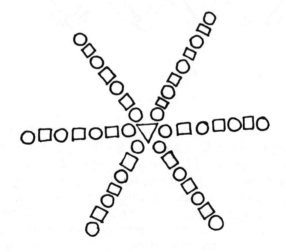

When the lines are big enough to be less than half the width of the rink's floor, have the girls skate outside of the line by the wall, and the guys toward the center of the rink. The FM will take of the guys' arms as they come to him. The line will go around in a circle as the FM turns around on one spot (Figure 30). At the sound of the whistle and toward the end of the record, each skater starts skating in a circle with the FM in the center, turning around. With each rotation, each skater skates faster and faster until the FM thinks that the lines are going fast enough. Then, he'll blow the whistle again to indicate the ending of the "wheel" and the Grand March. The DJ will announce "All Skate." The lines then can slow down and break up.

13

You Can Skate

Yes, YOU can skate if YOU want to. Roller skating can be learned like anything else. If you want to skate real good, you can do it. It's all up to you. You have to practice and continue practicing. Some people learn to skate faster than others, but if you want to skate and have fun, you can do it. You cannot learn by staying home or watching others.

You will fall down while roller skating, but in life, there are many ups and downs. They don't hurt physically like falling on skates, but the emotional falls of every day can do more damage and last longer than falls while skating. Bruises heal quicker than a nervous breakdown.

Also when you go to a roller rink, go to have fun. Please, don't carry a "chip" on your shoulder to spoil someone else's time. Remember, they may have problems that you might not even know of. By not pushing others to the "Breaking Point," maybe others won't push you to the "Breaking Point" so that you will not say something like, "Get off my back before my fist comes in contact with your face!"

With problems in this world, this is a good way to go and relax and have fun, while trying to think out your problems. Maybe by becoming friends with others or seeing some of your friends there, you will be able to share your troubles with others. And they can share their burden with you. If this should happen, please keep it to yourself because they are trusting you to do so. *A friend who tells everyone about everything that they know, is not a friend worth having.*

HAVE FUN.